Day of a Stranger

Day of a Stranger

Thomas Merton

Introduction by Robert E. Daggy

Gibbs M. Smith · Inc.
SALT LAKE CITY
1981

This is a Peregrine Smith Book.
Published by Gibbs M. Smith · Inc.

Copyright © 1981 by the Trustees of the Merton Legacy Trust.
All rights reserved. No portion of this book may be used or
reproduced by any means without written permission from
the publisher.
ISBN 0-87905-092-6
Library of Congress Number: 81-9153
Book design by Richard Firmage
Photograph of Thomas Merton (page 5) by Miguel Grinberg
Manufactured in the United States of America

First Peregrine Smith Edition

Introduction

Thomas Merton wrote "Day of a Stranger" in May 1965. It had been solicited and was not entirely a spontaneous production as were many of his journal writings. On the cover page of the third draft he noted in red ink: "These pages were written in answer to a request from a South American editor to describe a "typical day" in my life. The day was sometime in May 1965. Since then this has been rewritten & slightly amplified."

This typical day occurred when his life was undergoing a significant change, one for which he had hoped, prayed, worked and struggled. The change was his move to the hermitage, a concrete block structure in the hills above the Abbey of Gethsemani in Kentucky. Part-time at first, his stay there became much more full-time by the summer of 1965.

Though Merton carefully noted that "Day of a Stranger" was written as an *answer* to a request, there can be no doubt that he was glad to describe his life—his *new* life in the hermitage. He was exuberant about the move and, as his correspondence shows, anxious to tell his friends about it, to describe what it was like to him, to get his bearings for this hermit life as he told about it. Just weeks before he wrote "Day of a Stranger," he sent a letter to ex-Gethsemani monk, Ernesto Cardenal, then engaged in establishing a community in Nicaragua:

> I am living most of the time in the hermitage in the woods, sometimes eighteen hours out of the twenty-four, only coming down to the monastery for strict necessities and work in the novitiate. It is a wonderful life. Actually it has transformed me, and I am now at last convinced that I have found what I have always been looking for. Provided that it goes on this way.[1]

Merton's retirement was still incomplete in May, still very much an experiment. As he points out in "Day of a Stranger," he continued to have duties within the monastic community. Yet one can sense his excitement, his willingness to go on with the experiment, to carry it even further, to live in the hermitage where obligation ceased. A further step was taken in the summer of 1965, though total solitude remained compromised by requirements that he visit the monastery daily. He wrote to Cardenal in August:

> This week I will finally be able to leave the job in the novitiate...I have received permission to live entirely in the hermitage, coming down to the monastery only once a day to say mass and have one meal. This is a great step forward. I have in fact been sleeping there and spending most of my time there since last year, and have in fact had as much solitude as one would ordinarily have say in the Camaldolese. I find that it suits me perfectly.[2]

Merton's enthusiasm for this new life is clear. In "Day of a Stranger," he describes details of the life and of the hermitage—when it is cool, when it is hot—his problems with the outhouse (a bathroom and a chapel were not added till later), his campaign against insects. In this essay, in his letters and in his photographs as he became interested in photography, one can feel Merton's enjoyment of his life in the hermitage, his pride as it were in the hermitage itself. It became the closest thing to a home of his own that Merton had ever known. He wrote about it and he used the things in and around it as subjects for his camera. He tried, with his typewriter and with his camera, a new tool, to record clearly what was around him, what went to make up the fabric of his life.

[9]

He lovingly photographed the things he encountered in this life of solitude and contemplation. In this sense his camera truly became an instrument of contemplation. Merton says in this essay: "How I pray is breathe." His life was his prayer and the things in his life a part of that prayer—the trees, the sky, the grass, the hermitage. Even the plain and ordinary items he saw every day—the hermitage cross and wheel, the wheelbarrow, the chairs, the rain bucket, the typewriter—became a part of that prayer. Though he took photographs on his trips to Alaska, California, New Mexico and Asia, the majority were taken in Kentucky and most of those in the environs of Gethsemani. The bulk of the Gethsemani photographs were of the hermitage and its surroundings. Ultimately one gets closer to Merton and his life as he lived it in the last three years, to the everyday contemplative, the quasi-hermit, the stranger, through his photographs of Kentucky's knobs than through those of Asia's mountains.

"Day of a Stranger" fits into the pattern of Merton's journal writings. He recounts his thoughts and what outside influences may have been provoking them. He records what he was reading. He even tells us of quite ordinary routines. When he is finished, he leaves us feeling what his day was like. Though a description of just one day, "Day of a

Stranger" must be considered part of the sequence of autobiographical writings which includes *The Sign of Jonas, The Secular Journal, Conjectures of a Guilty Bystander,* the as yet unpublished *A Vow of Conversation (Diary 1964-1965), Woods, Shore, Desert: a Notebook— May 1968,* and *The Asian Journal.*

Merton was aware that his typical day was different from that of most people. His title, almost self-consciously, reflects the awareness that he was not typical. He happened to choose the word "stranger" in this case to emphasize his marginal and uncommon status. In other writings he uses different words to describe that status, but they become synonymous as he uses them: poet, bystander (sometimes innocent and sometimes guilty), alien, monk, the useless, the discontented, the unadapted. He was a stranger in part because his typical day failed to conform to modern United States society's conception of what a day should be. Yet his day was not chaotic, unscheduled, anarchical. There was always a definite routine. He is a stranger because he has withdrawn from society, or rather because he does almost nothing that society, as he sees it, considers respectable, acceptable and valuable. He refuses to be cast in a role that society finds comfortable and non-threatening, and because he rejects society's penchant for pigeonholing even though he knows he has been neatly pigeonholed, he becomes a stranger.

The essay, as Merton noted, was originally written for publication in South America. The word "stranger" may have been chosen for two reasons. He had already used stranger in other essays written for South America. He also knew that the essay would be translated into Spanish and that the translated title would be "Dia de un extrano." The Spanish word "extrano" conveys more of the feeling of being alien, of being extraneous, of not quite belonging to the world than does the English word "stranger."

"Day of a Stranger" is one of several essays which Merton wrote directly for South American publication. He did rework most of these for publication in the United States, but the impulse which prompted them was to communicate with Latin Americans. Many of the same themes run through these writings, one of which was Merton's desire to identify with Latin Americans, to convey that he was as much a stranger to the North American industrial-technological complex as were people in that part of the Third World. He read widely in Latin American literature. A substantial portion of his vast correspondence was with Latin American poets, editors, and social reformers, including Ernesto Cardenal, Pablo Antonio Cuadra, Miguel Grinberg, Sister Emmanuel de Souza e Silva, José Coronel Urtecho, Ludovico Silva, Margaret Randall de Mondragón, Esther de Caceres, Victoria Ocampo, and Napoleón Chow. The preface to *Obras Completas (Complete Works)*, "A Letter to Pablo Antonio Cuadra concerning Giants," "Message to Poets," "Answers on Art and Freedom" (originally subtitled "for Miguel Grinberg"), "Christian Humanism," "Answers for Hernan Lavin Cerda" (still unpublished in English) and others were conceived and written for South American audiences.

In "A Letter to Pablo Antonio Cuadra concerning Giants" Merton expresses regret at being a member of the exploiting society, the society of the giants of power and materialism. The "stranger" is a citizen of the Third World, a Latin American. The North American, Merton says, "cannot realize that the stranger has something very valuable, something irreplaceable to give him."[3] In a way then, in "Day of a Stranger," Merton goes one step further by identifying with those Third World strangers. He too is an alien, angrily saying in his first draft of the essay that he is not listened to by the same society which exploits Latin America.

Merton usually took a tone of apology for the United States and sympathy for Latin America in these essays. He disavowed the technological society of the United States while claiming kinship with the exploited and ignored strangers of Latin America. He consistently attempted to convey his sense of the innate integrity of the area. He stated in the Preface to the first (and so far only) volume of his *Obras Completas,* published in Argentina in 1960:

> I cannot be a "Northamerican" who knows only the rivers, the plains, the mountains and the cities of the north, the north where already there are no Indians, where the land was colonized and cultivated by Puritans, where, under the audacious and sarcastic splendor of the skyscrapers, one rarely sees the Cross and where the Holy Virgin, when she is represented at all, is pale and melancholy and carries no Child in her arms... It seems to me that I have heard the voice of all the hemisphere in the silence of my monastery, a voice that speaks from the depth of my being, with a clarity at once magnificent and terrible: as if I had in the depths of my heart the vast and solitary pampas, the brilliant hoarfrost of the Bolivian plateau, the thin air of the terraced valleys of the Incas, the splendor and suavity of Quito, the cold plains of Bogotá, and the intolerably mysterious jungles of the Amazon.[4]

His very fervor, the example of his life, the almost mystical quality of the empathy he claimed with South America without visiting it, save Merton from seeming patronizing. Somehow he managed not to come across as another American saying "Aren't you people wonderful and aren't Americans ugly?" He urged Latin Americans not to become like North Americans, to retain their own heritage and sense of difference.

Merton was convinced, and he based this conviction on wide reading, that Americans of the United States had dismissed rich and viable cultures. As he put it: "They have never awakened to the fact that Latin America is by and large culturally superior to the United States."[5] In this sense he sided with whole nations of strangers who were consciously and methodically being kept outside the mainstream of North American technology and material achievement. Yet he also let them know that he had to struggle to remain a stranger. In "Answers on Art and Freedom," he tells Grinberg:

> I do not consider myself integrated in the war-making society in which I live, but the problem is that this society *does* consider *me* integrated in it ... I have been simply living where I am and developing in my own way without consulting the public about it since it is none of the public's business.[6]

It is difficult to be a stranger. The great technological machine may treat some, like Latin Americans, as strangers, but ultimately most are sucked in. One must consciously choose to be a stranger in many ways. Merton repeats in "Day of a Stranger" that it is no one's business how he lives or where, but he writes that it takes effort to refuse the messages of the world to which one has chosen to be estranged.

He wrote in "Answers for Hernan Lavin Cerda" that technology is a fact and a necessity of modern life."[7] In his Latin American essays, he let his audience know that even he cannot get away from technology, from the messages it conveys to everyone, stranger or not. In "Day of a Stranger" the airplane theme runs throughout, a constant reminder to Merton of the bomb, of war, of a fast-paced, insane world beyond his Kentucky hills. He emphasizes with irony that the hills of Kentucky and Tennessee in fact become a refuge both for Merton the stranger and for the bomb, the force of destruction. Even in the monastery tractors "growl" and remind him of commercial endeavors, of making money, of materialism. One may live in seclusion but the modern world intrudes. One can only be a partial stranger. Though one has finally to come to grips with that world, it is important to maintain the stance and attitudes of the stranger.

One can refuse to participate directly. In "Message to Poets," Merton pleads: "Let us [poets] remain outside 'their' categories. It is in this sense that we are all monks: for we remain innocent and invisible to publicists and bureaucrats.'"[8] Yet he says that one can choose. "There is, in fact, a choice" to be invisible; intruded upon, yes, but consciously invisible. One can choose to a point to refuse the messages. One can refuse to be useful.[9]

These themes, repeated throughout his Latin American essays, appear in "Day of a Stranger," distinctly a part of this series of writings. Merton's first draft—short, terse, angry—described his day (though not much of it), but was essentially a variation on these themes. He deleted two passages, more screed than description, from the second draft. The first of these followed Merton's discussion of the ecology of the hermitage.

There is also the non-ecology, the destructive unbalance of nature, poisoned and unsettled by bombs, by fallout, by exploitation: the land ruined, the waters contaminated, the soil charged with chemicals, ravaged with machinery, the houses of farmers falling apart because everybody goes to the city and stays there.... There is no poverty so great as that of the prosperous, no wretchedness so dismal as affluence. Wealth is poison. There is no misery to compare with that which exists where technology has been a total success. I know these are hard sayings, and that they are unbearable when they are said in other countries where so many lack

[17]

everything. But do you imagine that if you become as prosperous as the United States you will no longer have needs? Here the needs are even greater. Full bellies have not brought peace and satisfaction but dementia, and in any case not all the bellies are full either. But the dementia is the same for all.[10]

Everyone, whether stranger or not, useless or useful, comes under the influence of that dementia. Merton continued this theme into the original ending. In that ending the stranger becomes first a political prisoner and finally, once again, the poet trying desperately to overcome the isolation which inevitably becomes the poet-stranger's state.

Soon I will cut bread, eat supper, say psalms, sit in the back room as the sun sets, as the birds sing outside the window, as silence descends on the valley, as night descends. As night descends on a nation intent upon ruin, upon destruction, blind, deaf to protest, crafty, powerful, unintelligent. It is necessary to be alone, to be not part of this, to be in the exile of silence, to be in a manner of speaking a political prisoner. No matter where in the world he may be, no matter what may be his power of protest, or his means of expression, the poet finds himself ultimately where I am. Alone, silent, with the obligation of being very careful not to say what he does not mean, not to let himself be persuaded to say merely what another

[18]

wants him to say, not to say what his own past work has led others to expect him to say.

The poet has to be free from everyone else, and first of all from himself, because it is through this "self" that he is captured by others. Freedom is found under the dark tree that springs up in the center of night and of silence, the paradise tree, the axis mundi, which is also the Cross.[11]

Merton reworked this first draft—which was barely four pages long. He deleted the above passages and expanded the essay to eight and one-half pages. The essay underwent a transformation between the first and second drafts. It became less angry, softer in tone, more a description of his day—became in fact one of Merton's prose poems. He became less concerned with conveying *his* message of danger and destruction and more concerned with relating the messages he received during the day—much the same message, of course, but the mood shifts. The second draft contains only one passage removed by Merton from the third and final draft published in the United States. This passage is concerned with the stranger's refusal to be part of a world he does not approve and Merton says again that the stranger must live with this refusal, must be proud and arrogant about his "strangerness." The passage came after the line "There is, in fact, a choice."

[19]

I do not intend to belong to the world of squares that is constituted by the abdication of choice, or by the fraudulent choice (the mass-roar in the public square, or the assent to the televised grimace).

I do not intend to be citizen number 152037. I do not consent to be poet number 2291. I do not recognize myself as the classified antisocial and subversive element that I probably am in the file of a department in a department. Perhaps I have been ingested by an IBM machine in Washington, but they cannot digest me. I am indigestible: a priest who cannot be swallowed, a monk notoriously discussed as one of the problems of the contemporary Church by earnest seminarists, wearing bright spectacles in Rome.

I have not chosen to be acceptable. I have not chosen to be inacceptable. I have nothing personal to do with the present indigestion of officials, of critics, of clerics, of housewives, of amateur sociologists. It is *their* indigestion. I offer them no advice.[12]

Merton sent this second draft, including the above passage, to South America where "Dia de un Extrano" was published in a Caracas journal, *Papeles,* in July 1966. This same version has been republished in South America, the latest appearance in Buenos Aires in *Antimitomania* in 1979.

Sometime later, following his usual pattern of writing, Merton expanded the essay further, deleted the above passage, added some new material, most notably the "interview" in which he responds with monosyllables. This final third draft came to nearly eleven pages of typescript. It became, with literally no changes, the redaction published in English and the one used as the text of this book.

The problem of selecting photographs to illustrate a Merton essay, when he himself had not chosen photographs, seemed difficult, and probably a little presumptuous at first. However, reviewing the photographs made the task in fact easy. The text itself, because of Merton's vivid images, calls up mental illustrations. A photograph exists for nearly every word image in "Day of a Stranger." The focus in Merton's photographs tends to be much the same as the images in his personal writings, images such as trees, woods, hills, gardens, barns, all the things one finds in the Kentucky countryside. Merton's agrarian bias, emphasizing the country as the ideal spot for silence and solitude, shows through as plainly in his photographs as in his prose and poetry. While he was attracted to certain man-made objects, such as chairs, stools and baskets, his photographs even when concentrated on something man-made are suffused with nature. He did photograph architecture, but the features which intrigued him most were the apertures—doors, windows and arches. He uses architecture most frequently in order to see out, to see beyond, to come again to nature. One sees from inside to the trees and plants outside.

Hardly a photograph of Gethsemani and the hermitage and surroundings does not have a tree or a plant in it, often seen through a door or window, often almost indiscernible in the background, but still there. As one feels the woods and the trees in Merton's journal writings, so one feels *and* sees them in his photographs.

Merton was interested in pattern and texture. Shadows fascinated him. Many of his photographs—of roots, stumps, stools and chairs—focus as much on the shadow the object casts as on the object itself. His interest in texture and shadow dominates his photographs. His root studies, of which there seem to be hundreds, concentrate as much on texture and dark interstices as they do on shape. Wood, the product of trees, figured largely in his photographs. Barn wood, for example, often provided a background even when not emphasized itself. The hermitage, much photographed itself, also acted as a backdrop for photographs of other objects. One can almost feel the roughness of the concrete blocks in these photographs and sense what surrounded Merton in his last three years.

The overwhelming emphasis in Merton's photographs, and one which puzzled me at first, is on inanimate objects. He spoke of the birds, the squirrels, the foxes and the rabbits around the hermitage and the Abbey, but he did not photograph them. He made one rather extensive, and to my mind uninteresting, study of walking sticks (family *Phasmidae*) he found around the hermitage. Other than this study there is one photograph of a horse, two or three of dogs, and some of sacred cows in India. The probable explanation for this gap in his photographs, despite the kinship he felt with our non-human brothers and sisters, is that Merton lacked equipment, such as a telescopic lens, and unlimited time to sit camera in hand waiting for the right shot of a bird or animal.

Merton tried in "Day of a Stranger" to describe a typical day in his life. His photographs also describe his life and the selections here are a representative sampling of the kinds of photographs he took. One can feel through them what it was like for him to live secluded in the woods, how that seclusion helped him to crystallize his message and to realize in his last three years the most active and productive writing period in his life. One can feel the silence, the sounds and non-sounds in that silence, the strangerness. He used both his typewriter and his camera to describe the milieu of solitude.[13] His writings and his photographs were not uniformly great or even at times very good, but they all illustrate his life, they reflect what he saw, they illumine his prayer. When an essay is as good as "Day of a Stranger" and the photographs as good and as compatible as the ones selected here, that prayer becomes an unusual and renewing experience for all of us.

Robert Edward Daggy
Bellarmine College
December 1980

NOTES

1. Letter from Thomas Merton to Ernesto Cardenal, Trappist, Kentucky, April 24, 1965; Thomas Merton Studies Center, Bellarmine College.

2. Letter from Thomas Merton to Ernesto Cardenal, Trappist, Kentucky, August 15, 1965; Thomas Merton Studies Center, Bellarmine College.

3. *The Collected Poems of Thomas Merton* (1977): p. 387.

4. Preface to *Obras Completas de Thomas Merton* (Buenos Aires, Sudamericana, 1960). No draft in English survives; this version was translated from the Spanish by Robert E. Daggy. The Preface has been published in *Introductions East and West; the Foreign Prefaces of Thomas Merton;* edited by Robert E. Daggy (Greensboro, North Carolina, Unicorn Press, 1981).

5. "Letter to Pablo Antonio Cuadra concerning Giants," *The Collected Poems of Thomas Merton* (1977): p. 387.

6. "Answers on Art and Freedom," *Raids on the Unspeakable* (1966): p. 172.

7. "Answers for Hernan Lavin Cerda;" unpublished manuscript in the Thomas Merton Studies Center, Bellarmine College, p. 1. Published as "Una Sociedad que está Peligrosamente Enferma;" translated into Spanish and edited by Hernan Lavin Cerda; *Punto Final* (Santiago de Chile) 2 (September 15, 1967): no. 37, pp. 14-16.

8. "Message to Poets," *Raids on the Unspeakable* (1966): p. 158.

9. This is the thrust of the essay "Answers for Hernan Lavin Cerda."

10. "Day of a Stranger;" first draft. Typescript in the Thomas Merton Studies Center, Bellarmine College, p. 2.

11. *Ibid.,* p. 4.

12. "Day of a Stranger;" second draft. Typescript in the Thomas Merton Studies Center, Bellarmine College, pp. 1-2.

13. For further elaboration on this theme, see the essay "Love and Solitude" in *Love and Living* (1979): pp. 15-24.

Day of a Stranger

The hills are blue and hot. There is a brown, dusty field in the bottom of the valley. I hear a machine, a bird, a clock. The clouds are high and enormous. Through them the inevitable jet plane passes: this time probably full of passengers from Miami to Chicago. What passengers? This I have no need to decide. They are out of my world, up there, busy sitting in their small, isolated, arbitrary lounge that does not even seem to be moving—the lounge that somehow unaccountably picked them up off the earth in Florida to suspend them for a while with timeless cocktails and then let them down in Illinois. The suspension of modern life in contemplation that *gets you somewhere!*

There are also other worlds above me. Other jets will pass over, with other contemplations and other modalities of intentness.

[30]

I have seen the SAC plane, with the bomb in it, fly low over me and I have looked up out of the woods directly at the closed bay of the metal bird with a scientific egg in its breast! A womb easily and mechanically opened! I do not consider this technological mother to be the friend of anything I believe in. However, like everyone else, I live in the shadow of the apocalyptic cherub. I am surveyed by it, impersonally. Its number recognizes my number. Are these numbers preparing at some moment to coincide in the benevolent mind of a computer? This does not concern me, for I live in the woods as a reminder that I am free not to be a number.

There is, in fact, a choice.

*

In an age where there is much talk about "being yourself" I reserve to myself the right to forget about being myself, since in any case there is very little chance of my being anybody else. Rather it seems to me that when one is too intent on "being himself" he runs the risk of impersonating a shadow.

Yet I cannot pride myself on special freedom, simply because I am living in the woods. I am accused of living in the woods like Thoreau instead of living in the desert like St. John the Baptist. All I can answer

[32]

is that I am not living "like anybody." Or "unlike anybody." We all live somehow or other, and that's that. It is a compelling necessity for me to be free to embrace the necessity of my own nature.

I exist under trees. I walk in the woods out of necessity. I am both a prisoner and an escaped prisoner. I cannot tell you why, born in France, my journey ended here in Kentucky. I have considered going further, but it is not practical. It makes no difference. Do I have a "day"? Do I spend my "day" in a "place"? I know there are trees here. I know there are birds here. I know the birds in fact very well, for there are precise pairs of birds (two each of fifteen or twenty species) living in the immediate area of my cabin. I share this particular place with them: we form an ecological balance. This harmony gives the idea of "place" a new configuration.

As to the crows, they form part of a different pattern. They are vociferous and self-justifying, like humans. They are not two, they are many. They fight each other and the other birds, in a constant state of war.

*

[34]

There is a mental ecology, too, a living balance of spirits in this corner of the woods. There is room here for many other songs besides those of birds. Of Vallejo, for instance. Or Rilke, or René Char, Montale, Zukofsky, Ungaretti, Edwin Muir, Quasimodo or some Greeks. Or the dry, disconcerting voice of Nicanor Parra, the poet of the sneeze. Here also is Chuang Tzu whose climate is perhaps most the climate of this silent corner of woods. A climate in which there is no need for explanation. Here is the reassuring companionship of many silent Tzu's and Fu's; Kung Tzu, Lao Tzu, Meng Tzu, Tu Fu. And Hui Neng. And Chao-Chu. And the drawings of Sengai. And a big graceful scroll from Suzuki. Here also is a Syrian hermit called Philoxenus. An Algerian cenobite called Camus. Here is heard the clanging prose of Tertullian, with the dry catarrh of Sartre. Here the voluble dissonances of Auden, with the golden sounds of John of Salisbury. Here is the deep vegetation of that more ancient forest in which the angry birds, Isaias and Jeremias, sing. Here should be, and are, feminine voices from Angela of Foligno to Flannery O'Connor, Theresa of Avila, Juliana of Norwich, and, more personally and warmly still, Raissa Maritain. It is good to choose the voices that will be heard in these woods, but they also choose them-

[36]

selves, and send themselves here to be present in this silence. In any case, there is no lack of voices.

*

The hermit life is cool. It is a life of low definition in which there is little to decide, in which there are few transactions or none, in which there are no packages to be delivered. In which I do not bundle up packages and deliver them to myself. It is not intense. There is no give and take of questions and answers, problems and solutions. Problems begin down the hill. Over there under the water tower are the solutions. Here there are woods, foxes. Here there is no need for dark glasses. "Here" does not even warm itself up with references to "there." It is just a "here" for which there is no "there." The hermit life is that cool.

The monastic life as a whole is a hot medium. Hot with words like "must," "ought" and "should." Communities are devoted to high definition projects: "making it all clear!" The clearer it gets the clearer it has to be made. It branches out. You have to keep clearing the branches. The more branches you cut back the more branches grow. For one you cut you get three more. On the end of each branch is a big bushy question mark. People are running all around with packages

[38]

of meaning. Each is very anxious to know whether all the others have received the latest messages. Has someone else received a message that he has not received? Will they be willing to pass it on to him? Will he understand it when it is passed on? Will he have to argue about it? Will he be expected to clear his throat and stand up and say "Well the way I look at it St. Benedict said...?" Saint Benedict saw that the best thing to do with the monastic life was to cool it but today everybody is heating it up. Maybe to cool it you have to be a hermit. But then they will keep thinking that *you* have got a special message. When they find out you haven't...Well, that's their worry, not mine.

*

This is not a hermitage — it is a house. ("Who was that hermitage I seen you with last night?...") What I wear is pants. What I do is live. How I pray is breathe. Who said Zen? Wash out your mouth if you said Zen. If you see a meditation going by, shoot it. Who said "Love?" Love is in the movies. The spiritual life is something that people worry about when they are so busy with something else they think they ought to be spiritual. Spiritual life is guilt. Up here in the woods is seen the New Testament: that is to say, the wind comes through the trees and you breathe it. Is it supposed to be clear? I am not inviting anybody to try it. Or suggesting that one day the message will come saying NOW. That is none of my business.

*

I am out of bed at two-fifteen in the morning, when the night is darkest and most silent. Perhaps this is due to some ailment or other. I find myself in the primordial lostness of night, solitude, forest, peace, a mind awake in the dark, looking for a light, not totally reconciled to being out of bed. A light appears, and in the light an ikon. There is now in the large darkness a small room of radiance with psalms in it. The psalms grow up silently by themselves without effort like plants in this light which is favorable to them. The plants hold themselves up on stems which have a single consistency, that of mercy, or rather great mercy. *Magna misericordia.* In the formlessness of night and silence a word then pronounces itself: Mercy. It is surrounded by other words of lesser consequence: "destroy iniquity" "wash me" "purify" "I know my iniquity." *Peccavi.* Concepts without interest in the world of business, war, politics, culture, etc. Concepts also often without interest to ecclesiastics.

Other words: Blood. Guile. Anger. The way that is not good. The way of blood, guile, anger, war.

Out there the hills in the dark lie southward. The way over the hills is blood, guile, dark, anger, death: Selma, Birmingham, Mississippi. Nearer than these, the atomic city, from which each day a freight car of

[44]

fissionable material is brought to be laid carefully beside the gold in the underground vault which is at the heart of this nation.

"Their mouth is the opening of the grave; their tongues are set in motion by lies; their heart is void."

Blood, lies, fire, hate, the opening of the grave, void. Mercy, great mercy.

The birds begin to wake. It will soon be dawn. In an hour or two the towns will wake, and men will enjoy everywhere the great luminous smiles of production and business.

*

[46]

_____ Why live in the woods?

_____ Well, you have to live somewhere.

_____ Do you get lonely?

_____ Yes, sometimes.

_____ Are you mad at people?

_____ No.

_____ Are you mad at the monastery?

_____ No.

_____ What do you think about the future of monasticism?

_____ Nothing. I don't think about it.

_____ Is it true that your bad back is due to Yoga?

_____ No.

_____ Is it true that you are practising Zen in secret?

_____ Pardon me, I don't speak English.

*

[48]

All monks, as is well known, are unmarried, and hermits more unmarried than the rest of them. Not that I have anything against women. I see no reason why a man can't love God and a woman at the same time. If God was going to regard women with a jealous eye, why did he go and make them in the first place? There is a lot of talk about a married clergy. Interesting. So far there has not been a great deal said about married hermits. Well, anyway, I have the place full of ikons of the Holy Virgin.

One might say I had decided to marry the silence of the forest. The sweet dark warmth of the whole world will have to be my wife. Out of the heart of that dark warmth comes the secret that is heard only in silence, but it is the root of all the secrets that are whispered by all the lovers in their beds all over the world. So perhaps I have an obligation to preserve the stillness, the silence, the poverty, the virginal point of pure nothingness which is at the center of all other loves. I attempt to cultivate this plant without comment in the middle of the night and water it with psalms and prophecies in silence. It becomes the most rare of all the trees in the garden, at once the primordial paradise tree, the *axis mundi,* the cosmic axle, and the Cross. *Nulla silva talem profert.* There is only one such tree. It cannot be multiplied. It is not interesting.

[49]

[50]

*

It is necessary for me to see the first point of light which begins to be dawn. It is necessary to be present alone at the resurrection of Day, in the blank silence when the sun appears. In this completely neutral instant I receive from the Eastern woods, the tall oaks, the one word "DAY," which is never the same. It is never spoken in any known language.

*

Sermon to the birds: "Esteemed friends, birds of noble lineage, I have no message to you except this: be what you are: be *birds*. Thus you will be your own sermon to yourselves!"

Reply: "Even this is one sermon too many!"

*

[52]

Rituals. Washing out the coffee pot in the rain bucket. Approaching the outhouse with circumspection on account of the king snake who likes to curl up on one of the beams inside. Addressing the possible king snake in the outhouse and informing him that he should not be there. Asking the formal ritual question that is asked at this time every morning: "Are you in there, you bastard?"

*

More rituals. Spray bedroom (cockroaches and mosquitoes). Close all the windows on south side (heat). Leave windows open on north and east sides (cool). Leave windows open on west side until maybe June when it gets very hot on all sides. Pull down shades. Get water bottle. Rosary. Watch. Library book to be returned.

It is time to visit the human race.

*

[54]

I start out under the pines. The valley is already hot. Machines out there in the bottoms, perhaps planting corn. Fragrance of the woods. Cool west wind under the oaks. Here is the place on the path where I killed a copperhead. There is the place where I saw the fox run daintily and carefully for cover carrying a rabbit in his mouth. And there is the cement cross that, for no reason, the novices rescued from the corner of a destroyed wall and put up in the woods: people imagine someone is buried there. It is just a cross. Why should there not be a cement cross by itself in the middle of the woods?

A squirrel is kidding around somewhere overhead in midair. Tree to tree. The coquetry of flight.

I come out into the open over the hot hollow and the old sheep barn. Over there is the monastery, bugging with windows, humming with action.

The long yellow side of the monastery faces the sun on a sharp rise with fruit trees and beehives. This is without question one of the least interesting buildings on the face of the earth. However, in spite of the most earnest efforts to deprive it of all character and keep it ugly, it is surpassed in this respect by the vast majority of other monasteries. It is so completely plain that it ends, in spite of itself, by being at least

[56]

simple. A lamentable failure of religious architecture—to come so close to non-entity and yet not fully succeed! I climb sweating into the novitiate, and put down my water bottle on the cement floor. The bell is ringing. I have duties, obligations, since here I am a monk. When I have accomplished these, I return to the woods where I am nobody. In the choir are the young monks, patient, serene, with very clear eyes, then, reflective, gentle, confused. Today perhaps I tell them of Eliot's *Little Gidding,* analyzing the first movement of the poem ("Midwinter spring is its own season"). They will listen with attention thinking that some other person is talking to them about some other poem.

*

[58]

Chanting the *alleluia* in the second mode: strength and solidity of the Latin, seriousness of the second mode, built on the *Re* as though on a sacrament, a presence. One keeps returning to the *re* as to an inevitable center. *Sol-Re, Fa-Re, Sol-Re, Do-Re.* Many other notes in between, but suddenly one hears only the one note. *Consonantia:* all notes, in their perfect distinctness, are yet blended in one. (Through a curious oversight Gregorian chant has continued to be sung in this monastery. But not for long.)

*

In the refectory is read a message of the Pope, denouncing war, denouncing the bombing of civilians, reprisals on civilians, killing of hostages, torturing of prisoners (all in Vietnam). Do the people of this country realize who the Pope is talking about? They have by now become so solidly convinced that the Pope never denounces anybody but Communists that they have long since ceased to listen. The monks seem to know. The voice of the reader trembles.

*

[60]

In the heat of noon I return with the water bottle freshly filled, through the cornfield, past the barn under the oaks, up the hill, under the pines, to the hot cabin. Larks rise out of the long grass singing. A bumblebee hums under the wide shady eaves.

I sit in the cool back room, where words cease to resound, where all meanings are absorbed in the *consonantia* of heat, fragrant pine, quiet wind, bird song and one central tonic note that is unheard and unuttered. This is no longer a time of obligations. In the silence of the afternoon all is present and all is inscrutable in one central tonic note to which every other sound ascends or descends, to which every other meaning aspires, in order to find its true fulfillment. To ask when the note will sound is to lose the afternoon: it has already sounded, and all things now hum with the resonance of its sounding.

*

I sweep. I spread a blanket out in the sun. I cut grass behind the cabin. I write in the heat of the afternoon. Soon I will bring the blanket in again and make the bed. The sun is over-clouded. The day declines. Perhaps there will be rain. A bell rings in the monastery. A devout Cistercian tractor growls in the valley. Soon I will cut bread, eat supper, say psalms, sit in the back room as the sun sets, as the birds sing outside the window, as night descends on the valley. I become surrounded once again by all the silent Tzu's and Fu's (men without office and without obligation). The birds draw closer to their nests. I sit on the cool straw mat on the floor, considering the bed in which I will presently sleep alone under the ikon of the Nativity.

Meanwhile the metal cherub of the apocalypse passes over me in the clouds, treasuring its egg and its message.